Real People

Amelia Earhart

By Philip Abraham

Welcome
Books

Children's Press®
A Division of Scholastic Inc.
New York / Toronto / London / Auckland / Sydney
Mexico City / New Delhi / Hong Kong
Danbury, Connecticut

Photo Credits: Cover, pp. 13, 15, 19 © Hulton/Archive by Getty Images;
pp. 5, 7, 11, 17, 21 © Bettmann/Corbis; p. 9 © Hulton-Deutsch Collection/Corbis

Contributing Editor: Jennifer Silate
Book Design: Christopher Logan

Library of Congress Cataloging-in-Publication Data

Abraham, Philip, 1970—
    Amelia Earhart / by Philip Abraham.
        p. cm. — (Real people)
    Includes bibliographical references and index.
    Summary: An easy-to-read biography of the female aviator who was the first woman to fly
alone across the country.
    ISBN 0-516-23952-X (lib. bdg.) — ISBN 0-516-23600-8 (pbk.)
    1. Earhart, Amelia, 1897—1937—Juvenile literature. 2. Air pilots—United States—Biography—
Juvenile literature. [1. Earhart, Amelia, 1897—1937. 2. Air pilots. 3. Women—Biography.] I. Title. II.
Real people (Children's Press)

    TL540.E3 A63 2002
    629.13'092—dc21
    [B]
                                                                                    2001042359

Contents

Meet Amelia Earhart.

She was a **pilot**.

5

Amelia started flying when she was twenty-three years old.

She worked hard to learn how to fly.

Amelia loved flying.

She even bought
her own plane.

Amelia was the first woman to fly alone across the Atlantic Ocean.

11

Amelia set many flying **records**.

Amelia also received many **awards** for her flying.

15

Amelia taught many people about flying.

Amelia also wrote books about her airplane trips.

She was very **famous**.

In 1937, Amelia **disappeared** while trying to fly around the world.

No one knows what happened to her.

We will always remember Amelia Earhart.

21

New Words

awards (uh-**wordz**) prizes for doing something well

disappeared (**diss**-uh-**pihrd**) having passed out of sight; gone

famous (**fay**-muhss) very well known

pilot (**pye**-luht) a person who flies an aircraft

records (**rek**-urds) the highest scores, rates, or speeds ever reached

To Find Out More

Books
Amelia Earhart: Pioneer of the Sky
by John Parlin
Dell Publishing

Young Amelia Earhart: A Dream to Fly
by Sarah Alcott
Troll Communications

Web Site
Amelia Earhart Museum
http://www.ameliaearhartmuseum.org/
On this site, you can read Amelia Earhart's biography and news clips about her adventures. There is also a tour of her childhood home, which is now a museum.

Index

About the Author
Philip Abraham is a freelance writer. He works in New York City.

Reading Consultants
Kris Flynn, Coordinator, Small School District Literacy, The San Diego County Office of Education

Shelly Forys, Certified Reading Recovery Specialist, W.J. Zahnow Elementary School, Waterloo, IL

Sue McAdams, Former President of the North Texas Reading Council of the IRA, and Early Literary Consultant, Dallas, TX